THE
ATLAS *of*
Endangered
ANIMALS

🌸 Belitha Press

First published in the UK in 1993 by
Belitha Press Limited
31 Newington Green, London N16 9PU
Reprinted 1993
Copyright in this format © Belitha Press 1993
Text copyright © Steve Pollock 1993
Illustrations copyright © Belitha Press 1993
Cartography copyright © Creative Cartography 1989
Edited and Designed by
The Book Creation Company, London
Black and white illustrations by Jackie Graham
Colour illustrations by Lynda Arnold
Printed in Singapore for Imago

ISBN 1 85561 104 X

Picture acknowledgements
All pictures supplled by Oxford Scientific Films, except:
Doug Allan, p 56: Ardea, pp 17, 26, 34, 50, 52, 53, 58: J. A. Cash, p 28: Bruce
Colman, pp 4, 6, 12, 16, 20, 22, 24, 38, 44, 49: K. W. Frink, p 32: Udo Hirsch, p 32:
Hutchison, pp 5, 32, 38, 44, 46, 54: NHPA, pp 33, 53: Planet Earth Pictures, pp 24,
37: Survival Anglia, pp 28, 48: WWF, pp 33, 49

CONTENTS

INTRODUCTION

The world has changed over millions of years, and is still changing. Most of the plants and animals we see around us will change too – some species will die out and new species will take their place. Sixty five million years ago the dinosaurs became extinct, although no one knows why. Something brought about a great change in the world that caused these creatures to die. This kind of cycle is quite natural and over thousands or millions of years many animals become extinct. However, since humans have appeared on the Earth some animals have died out in a much shorter time. This is because people change the world too quickly for animals to be able to change with it.

▲ Hunting for sport has put many species of water bird under threat.

CHANGING ANIMAL WORLDS

One of the most devastating ways in which humans put pressure on wildlife is by changing their habitats. For example, by clearing land to grow crops or build houses. Most animals cannot live in such dramatically changed conditions and move away or die.

All nature lives in a kind of balance and each living

◄ All over the world, animals are in danger because their habitat is being destroyed. This forest in Bali is being cut down to build a golf course. Because tourists bring a lot of money to the country they seem more important than the local wildlife.

INTRODUCING COMPETITION

Humans may also wipe out certain animals by introducing others that compete with them for food or even kill the animals that were there first. If this happens on an island, there is nowhere for the original inhabitants to escape to, and they can quickly die out. Goats, dogs, cats, pigs and rats have all harmed the original wildlife on small islands, while mongooses introduced to get rid of snakes have become pests.

▲ The Passenger Pigeon became extinct in 1914.

thing depends on another for its survival: if there were not enough meat-eating animals to eat the plant-eaters, all the plants would be eaten. When people started hunting with guns they began to upset this balance. Soon they started hunting animals for sport, killing many more than they needed for food.

THE MODERN HUNTERS

There are other more modern forms of hunting – taking live animals from the wild for pets, zoos or scientific research. Animals such as parrots, monkeys, lizards and snakes are captured and sold across the world. Many more are hunted for parts of their bodies. The skins of leopards and cheetahs, for example, are used to make fur coats, while those of

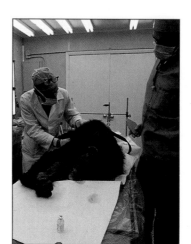

◄ Wild animals such as monkeys and apes are often used by scientists in their research.

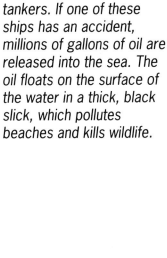

Many species of animal are endangered because they have been hunted for their skins. The most threatened are now protected by law, but animals are still killed to make fur coats.

Oil is transported around the world in enormous tankers. If one of these ships has an accident, millions of gallons of oil are released into the sea. The oil floats on the surface of the water in a thick, black slick, which pollutes beaches and kills wildlife.

crocodiles, alligators, lizards and snakes are turned into leather. The feathers of many exotic birds are also in great demand.

POLLUTION PROBLEMS

Today, people don't just live by hunting or growing food, they also use the Earth's resources to make things. Manufacturing these goods from raw materials can create further problems for ourselves and for wildlife in the form of pollution. Poisonous chemicals, such as pesticides, slowly get into animals' bodies through the air, the soil and the water, and eventually kill them.

In this rehabilitation centre in Sumatra, Orang-Utans that have been bred in captivity are reintroduced to life in the wild. The centre also allows tourists to see the animals without disturbing them.

▲ *Oil clogs up a sea bird's feathers so that they are no longer waterproof and cannot keep the bird warm.*

When travellers sailed to new lands, so did the rats, who lived on board the ships. The Brown Rat is now found in most countries, and in many cases, is a serious threat to local wildlife.

NATIONAL PARKS

National parks are officially protected areas that are very important for keeping wildlife safe. In these parks, the animals are living in their natural habitat and people can live alongside the wildlife too. Because these parks are so unspoilt and beautiful, people come and visit them to see the wildlife. The money that they bring is important because it goes towards keeping the parks running and helping to protect the wildlife from poachers.

DISTURBING ANIMALS' LIVES

People also sometimes harm animals by disturbing their lives and invading their homes. This has happened to the Manatee in the West Indies (see p.14) where not only is the sea becoming more and more polluted, but the animals often get caught up in fishing nets or may even be killed by speedboat propellers.

▲ Yellowstone is the oldest national park in the USA.

▶ In many countries, animals such as birds and monkeys are captured and taken from the wild to be sold as pets in local markets. Others are flown abroad for collectors.

HOW WE ARE HELPING ANIMALS

Although we have created so many problems for animals, we have also tried to help them. The Buffalo of the North American prairies would have been hunted to extinction if a group of people had not put some of them into a specially protected reserve.

Animals are often put into a safe place to breed, such as a zoo or reserve, which gives them the chance to build up their numbers. Not all people agree that a captive breeding programme (as this method is called) is the best way to save species, but when there are only a few animals remaining, it may be the only solution. Animals that have been saved from complete extinction in this way include the Arabian Oryx (see p.38) and the Hawaiian Goose.

If the breeding is successful, some of the animals may then be reintroduced into their natural habitat, but only if the original threat has been removed – sometimes the animal is safer if it stays in a reserve. Some of the pictures in this book were taken of animals in captivity, as many endangered species are very rare and hard to find in the wild.

◀ Imports of ivory are now banned in many countries but it is still in great demand and is very expensive. Even in protected national parks and game reserves, poachers kill the elephants and take their tusks.

MAKING MONEY OR SAVING ANIMALS?

Many of the countries where there are endangered animals are very poor, and local people make money by selling animals' skins or horns or by encouraging tourists to come and see the local wildlife. When an

▲ The animals in zoos are often bred in captivity.

animal has such a value to local people it may stand a better chance of surviving – if the people allow it to die out they will suffer, too.

In some countries, schemes have been set up to breed animals specially to help the local population. The main aim of these schemes is to make money, but they also help by reducing the numbers of animals that are hunted in the wild.

But saving species must not be simply about money. Humans must ensure that the world's wildlife remains unharmed for the benefit of the children of the future. We are as much a part of the natural world as the animals we share it with.

HOW TO USE THIS ATLAS

At the beginning of each animal entry there are three or four symbols that give information about the animal. For example, the symbols for the White-Tailed Sea Eagle are as follows:

The first symbol is a picture of that particular animal. This symbol is also used on the maps to show where that animal is found. You can use the symbol to find out where the animal lives. For animals that have become extinct, the map symbols show where it was last found before it died out.

The second symbol tells us whether the animal is rare, endangered, extinct, etc. This system has been set by the International Union for the Conservation of Nature (IUCN), who use eight categories, as follows:

 Extinct. No definite sighting of a species made in the wild in the last 50 years. Ex may be used to show that a species has recently become extinct.

 Endangered. Animals whose numbers are so low, or whose habitat has been so badly destroyed, that they will become extinct if nothing is done.

 Vulnerable. Animals that are still quite numerous, but are under great threat.

 Rare. Animals found only in one or a few places, or thinly spread over a larger area.

 Indeterminate. Animals known to be Endangered, Vulnerable, or Rare, but where there is not enough information to tell which group they belong to.

 Insufficiently Known. Animals thought to belong to the above categories, but for which too little information exists to be certain.

 Threatened. A term used for animals where there are several similar types – some in danger and some not.

 Commercially Threatened. Animals which are quite numerous, but which are being hunted. So far, this category has only been used for sea animals.

The next symbol shows how the animal came to be threatened. There are four symbols:

 Hunting. Animals hunted for sport, caught for the pet trade or killed for their skin or another part of their bodies.

 Habitat Destruction. This refers to the animal's natural surroundings being disturbed or destroyed by people.

 Pollution. Any form of pollution, from oil slicks to gradual poisoning from harmful chemicals in the soil, the water or the air.

 Competition. Where an introduced animal upsets the natural balance, either by killing other animals or by eating the food they depend on. A rat has been chosen for the symbol because it is a very common example of an introduced animal.

OTHER FEATURES OF THE ATLAS

Each map uses different colours to show different types of landscape and symbols to give you more information about a place:

Each colour map has various other features. There is a small locator map, showing where in the world that particular area is. There is also a compass, which tells you where that area is in relation to North, South, East and West. A small ruler tells you the scale of the map - that is, how many kilometres (or miles) one centimetre (or inch) across the map equals. Also, the colour maps have lines of latitude and longitude. These are imaginary lines used to divide the world up into smaller areas, and they are measured in degrees.

A R C T I C

GREENL
(Denmark)

ALASKA
(U.S.A.)

1

C A N A D A

2

UNITED STATES
OF AMERICA

BERMUDA

Tropic of Cancer

HAWAIIAN
ISLANDS (USA)

THE BAHAMAS

CUBA   HAITI   Puerto Rico (U.S.A.)
DOMINICAN
MEXICO   REP.   ANTIGUA AND BARBUDA
                    JAMAICA   ST. LUCIA
P A C I F I C   BELIZE   DOMINICA   ST. VINCENT
                GUATEMALA HONDURAS   BARBADOS
                EL SALVADOR   GRENADA   TRINIDAD AND TOBAGO
                    NICARAGUA   VENEZUELA
                    COSTA RICA   PANAMA
                            COLOMBIA   FRENCH GUIANA

Equator

                        GALAPAGOS   ECUADOR   SURINAM
NAURU   O C E A N   ISLANDS   GUYANA
                        (ECUADOR)
PAPUA   SOLOMON   KIRIBATI
NEW   ISLANDS   B R A Z I L
GUINEA   TUVALU   P
                                        E
            WESTERN   R
            SAMOA   U   BOLIVIA
VANUATU
        FIJI
                    TAHITI
            TONGA

Tropic of Capricorn   PARAGUAY

                PITCAIRN Is.
                (U.K.)   EASTER Is.
AUSTRALIA   (CHILE)

                                        URUGUAY

NEW ZEALAND   ARGENTINA

MIGRATION ROUTES

1 The Eskimo Curlew (see p22)
2 The Whooping Crane (see p22)
3 The Siberian Crane (see p 40)

Many birds that live in cold areas migrate to warmer areas for the
winter. The dotted lines on this map show the three longest migration
routes of birds featured in this book. Showing them on a map of the
world gives some idea of how migration patterns can endanger birds
that are hunted. The birds that travel through many countries are
more likely to lose vast numbers because they are hunted at every
stage of their journey. Also, they pass through different countries with
different laws. Just because an animal is protected in one country,
does not mean that it will be safe in another.

FALKLAND
ISLANDS

Antarctic Circle

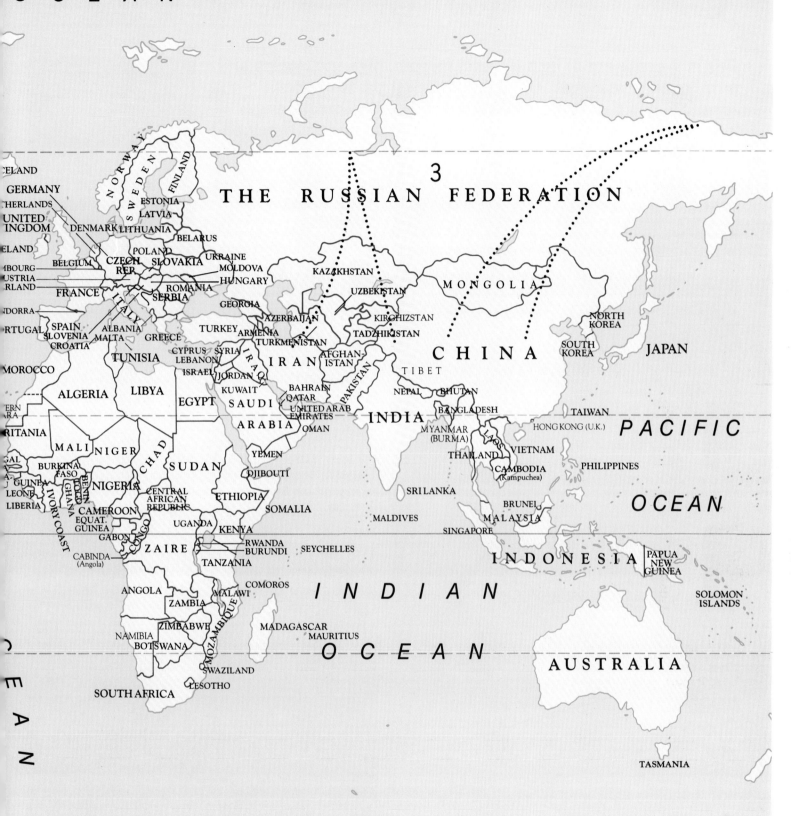

This is a continent of lush tropical forests, high mountains and wide, open grasslands. Of all the different parts of South America, it is the tropical forest which is in the most danger from highly destructive development, and so are the many and varied animals that live there.

◀ GOLDEN LION TAMARIN
Leontopithecus rosalia

Lion Tamarins are the largest members of the family of monkeys known as the marmosets and tamarins. There are three types of Lion Tamarin – the Golden Lion Tamarin, the Golden-Headed Lion Tamarin, and the Golden-Rumped Lion Tamarin. Probably only a few hundred of each species exist today in the wild, and they live only in the forests of Rio de Janeiro state, in Brazil.

During the 1950s, their numbers declined, as between two and three

▲ *Felling rainforests destroys animals' homes.*

hundred were taken from the wild each year for zoos, research or as pets. In 1971, the Poco d'Anta Biological Reserve was set up to the east of Rio, to help protect these beautiful monkeys and other threatened animals. A captive breeding programme organised by zoos throughout the world has also helped and numbers are now increasing, but their wild habitat is still threatened by agriculture.

MANED WOLF ▶
Chrysocyon brachyurus

This member of the dog family is not a wolf at all, but is in fact related to the fox. Its long legs help it to see over the tall plants of the grasslands and swamps where it lives. It feeds on a variety of animals, plants and fruit and will travel up to 32km (20 miles) looking for food.

The Maned Wolf's habitat is being destroyed and it is occasionally hunted. However, studies of the Maned Wolf in captivity suggest that it suffers from a variety of diseases, and this may pose the main threat to its survival.

80° 70° 60° 50° 40°

CARIBBEAN SEA

Barranquilla • Maracaibo • **Caracas**
Cartagena • Barquisimeto • Ciudad Guayana
10° PANAMA Cucuta Orinoco **Georgetown** **Paramaribo**
Bucaramanga VENEZUELA GUYANA **Cayenne**
Medellin Angel Falls SURINAM FRENCH
Bogota COLOMBIA Mt Roraima GUIANA
(9,094 ft/2,772 m)
Buenaventura Guyana Highlands
Cali
Esmeraldas Negro Macapa
Equator 0° **Quito** Mt Cotopaxi (19,344 ft/5,896 m)
ECUADOR Mt Chimborazo Fonte Boa Manaus Amazon Belem
(20,561 ft/6,272 m)
Guayaquil Iquitos Leticia Fortaleza
Cuenca
S e l v a s Madeira Natal
Chiclayo Rio Branco Xingu Recife
Trujillo PERU Porto Velho
Mt Huascaran Cobija BRAZIL Maceio
(22,205 ft/6,768 m)
10° Callao 10°
Lima PERU Salvador
Pampas Galeras Reserve Tocantins Campos
Cuzco Mato São Francisco
Lake Cuiaba Grosso
Titicaca BOLIVIA
La Paz Goiânia **Brasília** BRAZILIAN
Cochabamba
Santa Cruz Uberlandia Montes Claros
Sucre
Potosi HIGHLANDS
20° Iquique Campo 20°
Atacama Desert Grande
Paraguay Londrina Campinas Niterói
Antofagasta Salta G r a n Rio de Janeiro
C h a c o PARAGUAY Sao Paulo Tropic of Capricorn
Copiapo San Miguel **Asuncion** Coronel Curitiba
de Tucumán Parana Oviedo
Salado Uruguay **Iguacu**
Córdoba **National Park**
30° Parana Salto Porto Alegre 30°
Valparaíso San Luis Rosario Paysandú Rio Grande
Santiago Colorado **Buenos Aires** URUGUAY
River Bio-Bio La Plata **Montevideo**
Concepcion **ARGENTINA**
Mt Aconcagua P a m p a s
(22,831 ft/6,959 m)
Temuco Mar del Plata
Bahía Blanca

PACIFIC Colorado
OCEAN ATLANTIC
OCEAN
Puerto Montt GULF OF SAN MATÍAS

40° 40°

GULF OF
SAN JORGE
Comodoro
Rivadavia

N
W E
S

Patagonia

Falkland Islands
(Islas Malvinas)
(United Kingdom)

50° 50°
Punta Arenas Tierra Del
Fuego Cape Horn

80° 70° 60° 50° 40° 30° 20°

0 500 1000 1500 2000 2500 km
cm 1 2 3 4 5 6 7 8 9 10
inches 1 2 3 4
0 500 1000 1500 miles

▼ SPIX'S MACAW
Cyanopsitta spixii

This species of macaw lives in the north-eastern region of Brazil, in Bahia State. A survey in July 1990 found only one male macaw living in this area. He was trying to breed with a different species of macaw because there were no females of his kind left to breed with.

Probably the main reason for this bird's decline is netting for the captive bird trade. Between 1977 and 1987 at least 23 birds were handled by dealers. Another problem is that the trees they need to nest and roost in never get a chance to grow because goats and cattle eat them while they are still young, and the few nesting holes that remain are sometimes taken over by bees. Unless the Spix's Macaw is bred in captivity, it will certainly become extinct.

◄ GIANT ANTEATER
Myrmecophaga tridactyla

Millions of years ago, huge Anteaters, Sloths and Armadillos roamed the South American plains. They belonged to the group edentates ('toothless ones') and many died out when the sea level lowered.

The Anteater uses its tongue to eat ants and termites. However, termite nests are getting rarer as grasslands are given over to cattle, and this is reducing the anteater's food supply.

▲ GIANT OTTER
Pteronura brasiliensis

The Giant Otter lives in the waterways of the Amazon Basin. Like other otters, it has been hunted over the years for its soft fur. Around 2000 used to be exported from Brazil each year, and although it is now protected, the hunting goes on.

The Giant Otter is unusual in that its tail is flattened from top to bottom, rather than side to side like other otters. Their habitat has been disturbed by gold prospectors, and by people cutting down the tropical forests.

▼ JUNIN GREBE
Podiceps taczanowskii

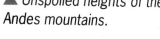

Lake Junin lies in the highlands of Peru, at an altitude of 4000m (13,000ft). Amongst the reed beds that shelter this large lake live about 100 Junin grebes.

Before 1961, the flightless grebe was quite common. But when copper mining started nearby, poisonous metals washed into the lake, and by 1979 much of the lake was dead. The grebes' only hope for survival is if the lake is turned into a reservoir for the city of Lima, and so has to be cleaned.

▲ VICUNA
Vicugna vicugna

In the sixteenth century there were millions of Vicuna living on the grasslands in the mountains of South America. By the 1950s, their numbers had dropped to around 400,000 and by 1969 there were so few left that they were placed on the endangered list. With full protection, they were moved to the vulnerable list in 1981, and today there are about 85,000 Vicuna living in central Peru, West Bolivia, north-eastern Chile and north-western Argentina.

This programme has been successful mainly because Vicuna fur is very valuable, so now the animals are ranched and farmed – an example of economic conservation.

▲ *Unspoiled heights of the Andes mountains.*

◄ ARAPAIMA
Arapaima gigas

This is one of the largest freshwater fish in the world today, growing to lengths of up to 2m (7ft). Unfortunately, this also means that the Arapaima makes an easy target for a bow and arrow. Large numbers are hunted and eaten and this is the main reason for its present decline.

Fish keep afloat with a swimbladder and 'breathe' through gills. The Arapaima is unusual as its swimbladder is connected to its throat, so it can take air in through its mouth as well as its gills. This is helpful in the dry season when water levels are low and water may be stagnant, with very little oxygen.

The main habitats of the countries of Central America are mountains and tropical forest and, as in other parts of the world, the forests are under threat.

On the Caribbean islands, some of the native animals are at risk because settlers introduced new animals which upset the natural balance.

 Peaceful coral shallows off the Belize coast.

▼ CUBAN CROCODILE
Crocodylus rhombifer

This crocodile lives only in the swampland of central Cuba, in the Cienaga de Zapata. No more than a few hundred remain there now and the area has been declared a sanctuary by the Cuban government.

The Cuban Crocodile grows up to 4m (13ft) long. It feeds on small mammals, fish and birds. Like alligators and many other species of crocodile, it used to be hunted for its skin, which can be used as leather.

▼ QUEEN CONCH
Strombus gigas

This large sea snail has always been hunted for food, but modern hunting methods mean that too many are being caught. People are now starting to farm conches, however, so the wild ones will not be harmed.

▲ MANATEE
Trichechus manatus

The West Indian Manatee belongs to a group of animals called sea cows. It lives in the coastal waters of the Caribbean, feeding on seaweed. It also lives in rivers, where it eats water hyacinths.

These gentle, slow-moving creatures spend all their time in the water, and have been easy prey for hunters who kill them to eat. This has reduced their numbers seriously, especially because they breed slowly – a female Manatee produces only one calf every two years.

Living in the coastal waters, Manatees may be affected by pollution and they are also in danger of being entangled in fishing gear, or hurt by the propellers of power boats.

However, since Manatees eat the water weed that clogs up irrigation canals and dams in the area, this may encourage people to protect them in the future.

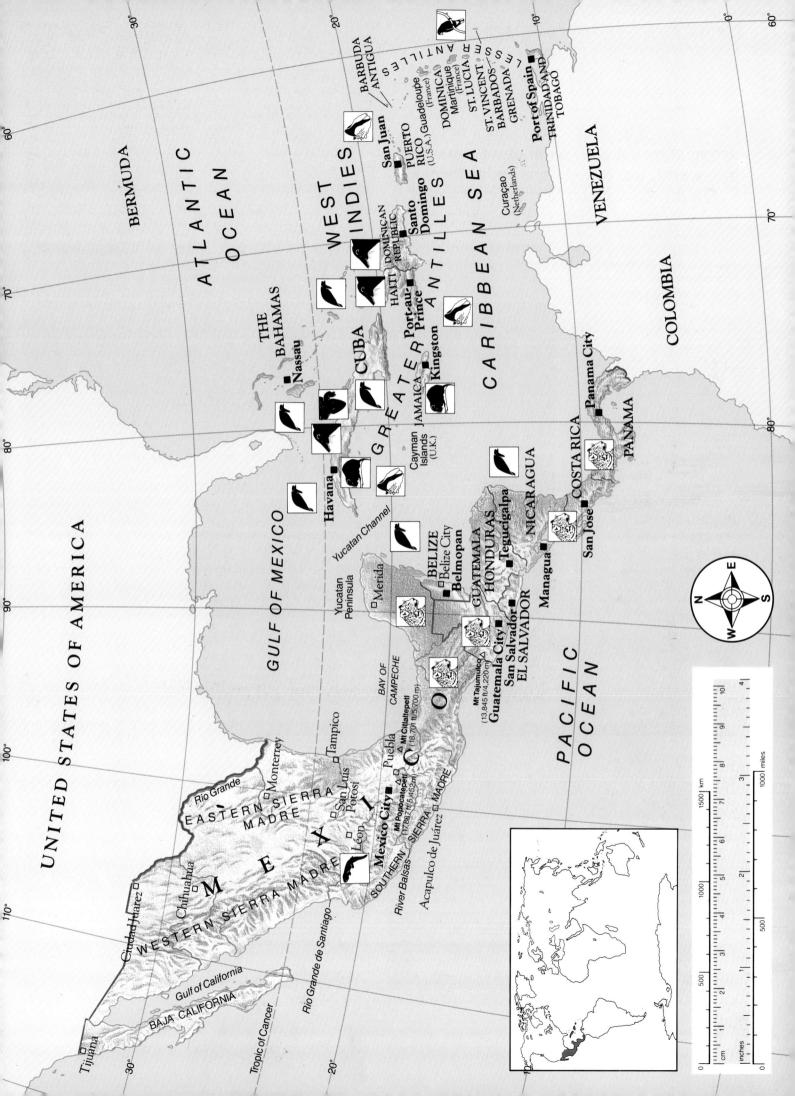

▲ AXOLOTL
Ambystoma mexicanus

Found only in Lake Xochimilco in Mexico, this unique amphibian is a type of salamander that never grows into an adult. Axolotls are in danger of being killed by water pollution, although they do have a secure future in captivity.

▼ JAGUAR
Panthera onca

The Jaguar used to be found all through Central and South America, but it is now extinct in El Salvador and facing extinction in Costa Rica and Panama. In Guatemala, southern Mexico and western Belize, however, it is increasing in number.

The number of Jaguars killed for their skin has fallen dramatically, as far fewer people today want to wear fur coats. This means that hunters cannot make money by killing Jaguars, and they leave them alone.

Jaguars feed on animals like capybara, agouti and caiman, but as these are hunted by loggers and other people living in the forests, their food supply is threatened. In some farming areas, Jaguars are hunted as pests because they kill cattle.

Despite this, the future of the Jaguar is quite hopeful and several countries are setting up wildlife reserves where they are protected.

◀ ST LUCIA AMAZON
Amazona versicolor

This parrot lives on the island of St Lucia in the Lesser Antilles. The islands are volcanic and also suffer from hurricanes, which causes problems for the tiny populations of parrots living there. In 1979, a volcano erupted on the island of St Vincent killing many of the highly endangered St Vincent Amazon and destroying their habitat.

With only 250 St Lucia Amazons remaining, a hurricane or volcanic eruption on the island could be disastrous. Fortunately, there are now captive breeding programmes at various zoos around the world. Even if there were a disaster and the wild population were reduced or destroyed, the parrots could eventually be reintroduced. The parrots are protected in the wild and are the island's national bird, so they have become a valuable tourist attraction.

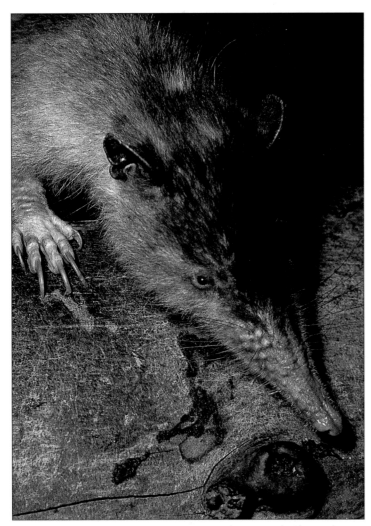

▲ Destructive burning of scrubland in Costa Rica.

▲ CUBAN AND HISPANIOLAN SOLENODON

Solenodon cubanus and *S. paradoxus*

Solenodons look rather like large shrews, and measure 50cm (20in) from nose to tail. The snout is long and flexible, and perfectly adapted for probing into crevices and leaf litter in search of the snails, crickets, beetles and small crabs that form their diet.

Unlike shrews, they live in family groups, in rock crevices and burrows in both moist and semi-dry forest. But this habitat is under threat from both deforestation and land development. Another threat is posed by domestic cats that have gone wild, and which are thought to kill solenodons for food.

The Cuban Solenodon probably has a better chance of survival than the Hispaniolan species, because the Cuban government has set up reserves for the solenodon as well as for the endangered Ivory-billed Woodpecker. Unfortunately, neither Haiti nor the Dominican Republic have made any effort to conserve the Hispaniolan Solendon, native to those islands.

▼ CUBAN AND JAMAICAN HUTIA

Capromys pilorides and *Geocapromys brownii*

These rodents are about the size of a rabbit. There used to be some 20 different species of hutia living on many of the islands of the West Indies, but they have long been a popular source of food for human beings and only a few species survive today. Remains of the extinct forms have been found in caves and other places that were used for human habitation.

The Cuban and Jamaican hutias live in trees, but they will come down to the ground and shelter in burrows if danger threatens.

They feed on animals such as lizards, as well as plants. Both species are in great danger of extinction, because they are eaten by animals that have been introduced to the islands, such as cats and mongooses.

Ever since the first settlers arrived nearly 400 years ago, people from all over the world have been exploiting the USA's wealth of land and natural resources.

Large areas of this vast, varied country have been developed for agriculture, industry or housing and pollution is a problem. The natural environment has been changed greatly, and the nation's wildlife has suffered as a result. However, there is a strong conservation movement in the USA – it was actually the first country to have national parks.

IVORY-BILLED WOODPECKER ▶
Campephilus principalis

No one is sure whether there are any of these birds left in the USA at all. It was never common because it lives on beetle grubs found only in the dead wood of large, old forests. The rise of the timber trade after the 1880s destroyed its only source of food.

By 1968 there were just six breeding birds in the USA. None have been found since, although today there are about four pairs living in Cuba.

▲ AMERICAN LOBSTER
Homarus americanus

Like shrimps and crabs, lobsters are part of an animal group called crustaceans. These crustaceans also belong to a food group – 'shellfish' – which is popular with people across the world. Before overfishing, lobsters grew to huge sizes – the largest weighed about 20kg (44lb) and was about 60cm (2ft) long. Coastal pollution has also reduced numbers.

▲ RED WOLF
Canis rufus

This type of wolf was once common throughout south-central America. Today, only about 300 red wolves survive – in one part of south-east Texas and the nearby Cameron Parish in Louisiana. One particular Texan sub-species became extinct as late as the 1970s.

An inborn but often mistaken human fear of wolves means that they are hunted down at every opportunity.

The survival of the Red Wolf is also threatened by its own behaviour. Red Wolves have been breeding with coyotes, which are also members of the dog family, and very common across America. As time goes by, the special features of the Red Wolf are being lost, and it is starting to look more and more like the coyote.

◀ CALIFORNIAN CONDOR
Gymnogyps californianus

This huge bird used to be found over a wide area of the USA, but it has been declining since the end of the last century and was even thought to be extinct in the 1930s.

Condors eat the carcasses of dead animals and this can cause problems in the modern world. The animals they eat may have been killed by hunters, using lead shot, which poisons the birds, or they may eat poisoned meat left out to kill coyotes. They also suffer from the use of pesticides, which make the shells of their eggs very thin, so their young die before they hatch.

The last condor was taken from the wild in 1987 and since then it has been bred in captivity. There are now 40 birds, but the problem is finding a suitable place to release them into the wild again.

GILA MONSTER ▶
Heloderma suspectum

The Gila Monster is one of only two species of venomous lizard in the world today. It is named after the Gila Basin in Arizona, where it lives. It moves slowly, and eats eggs and young birds, mice or rats.

It is now protected, but in the early 1950s it was very rare as vast numbers were collected as pets.

◀ HUMPBACK WHALE
Megaptera novaeangliae

The Humpback Whale belongs to the same group as the Blue Whale (see p.58). Both are found in all oceans, and both were nearly hunted to extinction. It has become one of the most closely studied whales, and is known for its underwater songs, which it uses to communicate over long distances.

In the USA, it has become a tourist attraction to travel in boats and watch these gentle giants feeding in coastal waters. Because money is to be made if the whales are kept alive, their future now looks more promising.

▲ *Nature has given way to polluted cities.*

▲ PADDLEFISH
Polyodon spathula

This strange fish lives in the Mississippi Valley. It feeds by collecting tiny plants and animals in its open mouth as it swims.

The Paddlefish is a living fossil. Remains have been found of similar fish from 100 million years ago. Today they are threatened by the building of dams and spreading pollution.

▲ *Intensive farming is destroying animals' habitats.*

▲ BLACK-FOOTED FERRET
Mustela nigripes

The Black-Footed Ferret has become an endangered animal because it is a fussy eater! Unlike the other kinds of ferret and polecats, it will only feed on Prairie Dogs. These are not really dogs, but rodents. They look like stocky ground squirrels, and live underground in burrows on the prairie.

When the prairies were truly wild, Prairie Dogs could dig large networks of burrows, called a town. The Black-Footed Ferret not only ate the Prairie Dogs but lived in their burrows too. Once the prairies were ploughed up for growing wheat, the Prairie Dogs were considered a pest, and their numbers were controlled. This meant that the Black-Footed Ferret's home and source of food were both threatened at once.

The only places where Prairie Dogs, and therefore Black-Footed Ferrets, can now survive undisturbed are a few national parks.

CANADA (including Alaska)

This is the second largest country in the world. Much of it is wild and uninhabited, but wildlife here still needs protection. The oil industry has created widespread pollution throughout Canada and Alaska. An area on the west coast, near Prince Rupert, was badly damaged by oil spilled from the *Exxon Valdez* tanker in the late 1980s. Oil covered the coast, killing sea otters and thousands of birds. It takes more than the passing of laws to protect animals from this sort of disaster.

POLAR BEAR ▶
Ursus maritimus

Polar Bears are found in six countries within the Arctic Circle, and all six have agreed that the bears should be conserved and managed properly, and that their environment should be protected.

The hunting of Polar Bears from aircraft and motor boats is banned by all six countries. However, some of them allow a certain amount of hunting, for the benefit of native peoples who have traditionally hunted bears. For example, Canada allows 600 bears to be taken each year, mainly for meat and for the sale of skins.

▲ WHOOPING CRANE
Grus americana

Of all cranes, this is the one closest to extinction. In the mid-1950s there were just 14 birds left in the wild. It breeds only in the Wood Buffalo National Park in Canada, then migrates south to the Gulf of Mexico. It is protected and is also being helped by a captive breeding programme.

◀ ESKIMO CURLEW
Numenius borealis

This bird was once so numerous that extinction seemed impossible. Flocks migrated from Canada to Chile, then back to Canada in spring.

They were hunted at every stage of their long journey and by 1900 few were left. By 1970 they were thought to be extinct, but in 1983, 23 birds were seen in Texas and there have been several sightings since.

▲ Canada's mixture of forest and frozen plain.

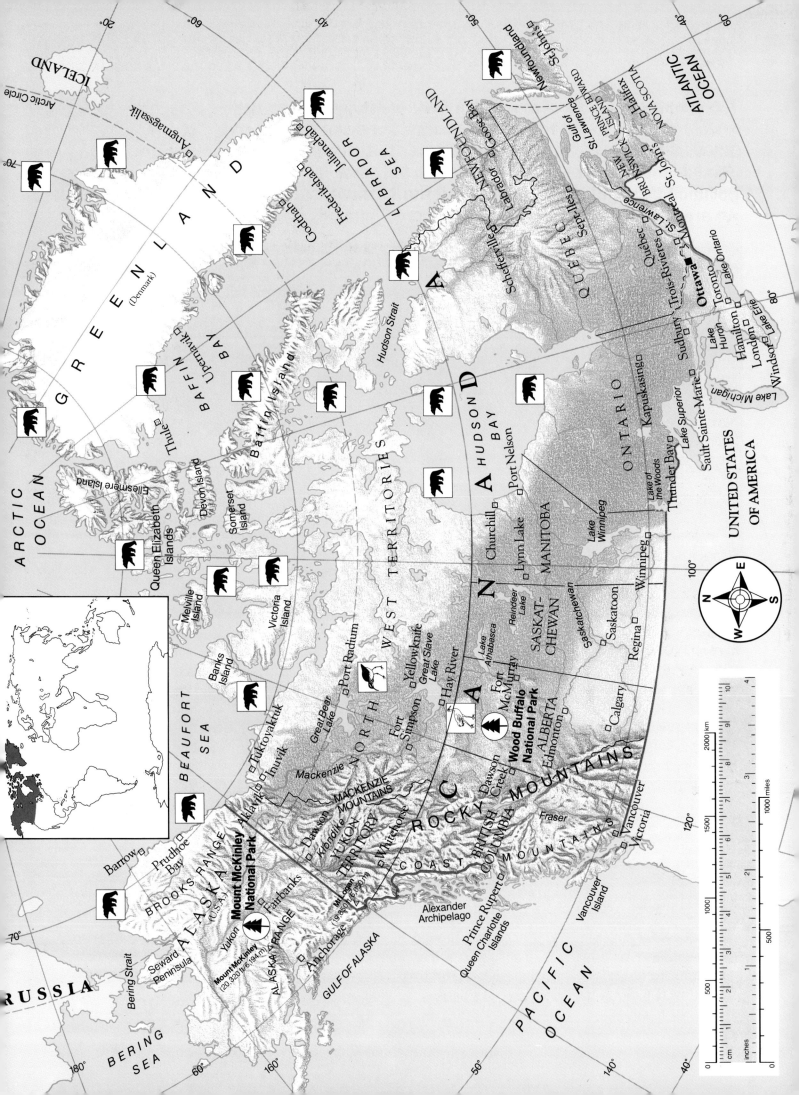

SCANDINAVIA

The countries in Scandinavia have very cold winters and the wildlife there is generally specialised for surviving these harsh months. The forests are dense, and trees that are cut down to make paper are replanted. Much of Scandinavia is mountainous, and Norway is famous for its spectacular fiords.

▲ Norway's fiords were formed in the last Ice Age.

◀ GREY WOLF
Canis lupus

In many European countries wolves have been deliberately hunted to extinction, simply because people were afraid of them. In Scandinavia, the Grey Wolf is almost extinct.

Six wolves were known to live in Sweden, and during the 1980s they bred in an area on the border with Norway. They had a chance for survival here, because enough food was available in the form of red deer and moose. But although it was against the law, people hunted them down and 9 of the 15 pups were killed.

▶ WHITE-TAILED SEA EAGLE
Haliaeetus albicilla

This is the largest European eagle, with its wing span of over 2m (6ft). The European population of White-tailed Sea Eagles is between 500 and 700 birds, and Norway is home to about half of them. With its hundreds of kilometres of undisturbed coastline, it provides plenty of nesting sites and food.

Because the eagle eats dead meat, sheep-rearing areas in the mountains of Europe must once have provided an ample source of food. Farmers there regarded the eagles as a threat to

their livestock, and so many were poisoned or shot. Sometimes eagles have been poisoned by accident. In Iceland, for example, many died from eating bait left out to kill Arctic Foxes. Numbers dropped to 150 pairs in 1880. A century later, there were just 20 pairs.

Today, pesticides are another threat. They make the shells of the eagles' eggs so thin that unborn chicks perish.

▼ WOLVERINE
Gulo gulo

The Wolverine is the heaviest member of the weasel family. It has a reputation as a powerful killer, as it can prey on animals much larger than itself, like deer.

Wolverine fur is much less valuable than it once was, so the animals are now less likely to be hunted. Numbers of Wolverines have gone down recently, but this does not seem as yet to be posing too great a threat to the species.

ICELAND

Vatneyri
Akureyri
Reykjavik
Vatnajokull
Hofn
Mt Hekla
(4,747ft/1,491m)
Mt Oraefajokull
(7214 ft/2199 m)

ATLANTIC
OCEAN

North Cape
National Park

BARENTS
SEA

Varanger Fjord

Alta

Lemmenjoki
National Park

Tromso

Lake Inari

Lapland

Vesteralen
Islands

Narvik

Lofoten
Islands

Mt Kebnekaise
(6,926ft/2,111m)

Kiruna

Bodo

N
O
R
W
E
G
I
A
N

S
E
A

Lulea

S
W
E
D
E
N

Skelleftea

Umea

GULF OF BOTHNIA

Vaasa

FINLAND

RUSSIA

Arctic Circle

N
O
R
W
A
Y

Mt Glitterlind
(8,110ft/2,452m)

Mt Galdhoppigen
(8103 ft/2470 m)

Trondheim

Dombas

Sundsvall

Tampere

Voss

Lillehammer

Bergen

Lagen

Glama

Turku

Helsinki

GULF OF FINLAND

Oslo

Notodden

Uppsala

Stavanger

Lake
Vanern

Lake
Malaren

Stockholm

Kristiansand

Norrkoping

Lake
Vattern

Linkoping

Skagerrak

Gothenburg

Boras

Gotland

Alborg

Kattegat

Oland

Jutland

Arhus

Helsingborg

Copenhagen
DENMARK

Esbjerg

Odense

B
A
L
T
I
C

S
E
A

Bornholm

NORTH
SEA

GERMANY

Oulu

500 km

cm   1   2   3   4   5   6   7   8   9   10

inches   1   2   3   4

400 miles

Most of the countries in this part of the world no longer have their original wild habitats. Over the years, the people living here have destroyed and changed much of it beyond recognition. Today the land is used for farming and developments such as factories, housing and road building. The spread of industries producing goods to sell gives rise to some pollution of the rivers and the air. All of this in turn affects the wildlife, putting much of it at risk.

▲ Pollution fills the air in Fawley, England.

◀ EUROPEAN OTTER
Lutra lutra lutra

This animal was once common over much of Europe, but is now very rare. In some countries, such as the British Isles, it has been given full protection, and can no longer be hunted for its soft, sleek fur.

They are easily disturbed, and prefer to live well away from people. Since they eat fish, water pollution harms otters. But even when they find clean rivers, their problems are not over. Some fishermen think that otters threaten their livelihood by eating valuable fish like salmon and trout, although research shows that otters prefer to eat eels.

▼ PARDEL LYNX
Felis pardina

This cat survives in Spain in the mountains of the Pyrenees, in Portugal and in the Coto Donana – a wetland area very different to the other mountainous habitats.

The Pardel Lynx is not a forest animal like the lynx of northern Europe. It prefers open pine woods or shrubby areas.

It hunts rabbits, young deer and game birds, such as the Red-legged Partridge. This has probably led to it being killed by gamekeepers. It may also have suffered a food shortage when a disease called myxomatosis was killing thousands of rabbits in the 1950s and 1960s. In the future, the lynx will only survive where it is well protected.

▲ SPUR-THIGHED TORTOISE
Testudo graeca graeca

This tortoise is particularly at risk, although all tortoises are threatened. This is because, for so many years, they have been sent to Northern Europe as pets. Many died on the journey, others perished in the cold climate because owners didn't know how to hibernate them properly. Importing tortoises has now been banned by many European countries, so their future looks better.

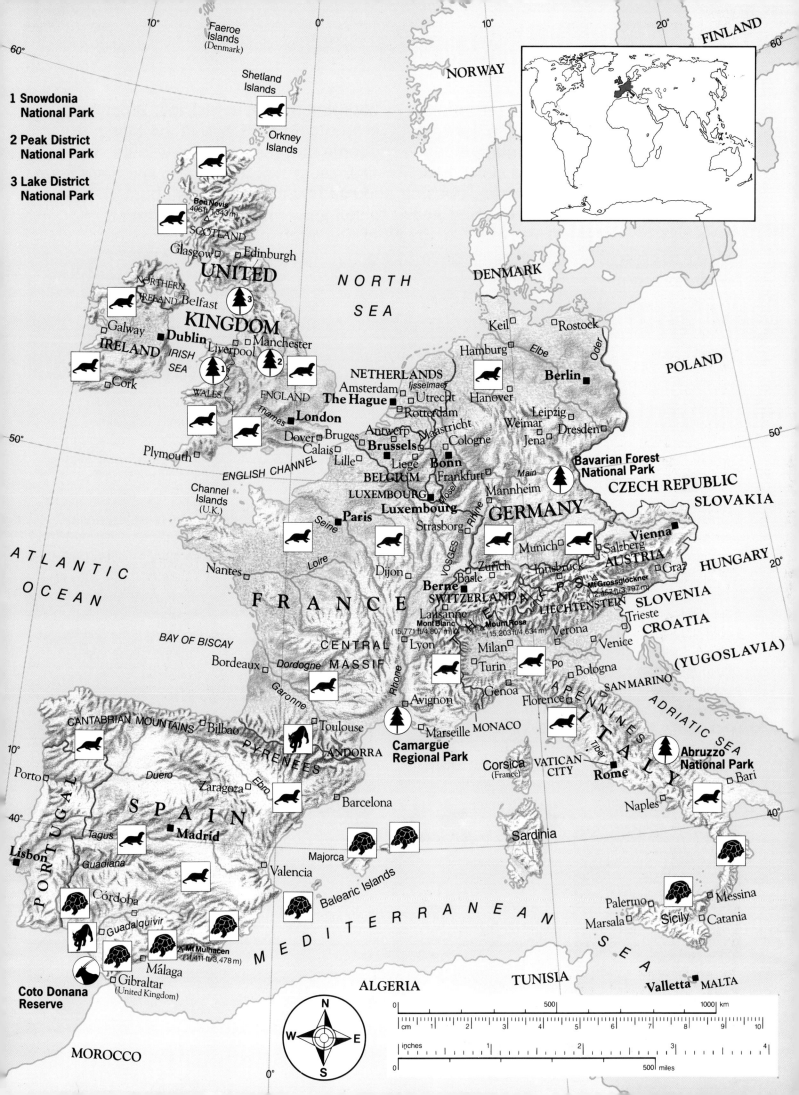

This part of Europe stretches from the warm climate of Greece in the south to the much cooler Poland in the north. Many of the countries in the north have problems with pollution from heavy industries. The ones in the south have booming tourist industries, which can create conflict between the needs of people and the needs of wildlife. The animals at risk in East Europe have been endangered by these two human activities – tourism and pollution.

DALMATIAN PELICAN ▶
Pelecanus crispus

This is the largest pelican, and the most endangered, but five thousand years ago it was widespread across Europe. Even in 1873, there were millions in Romania but numbers dropped to thousands in just 20 years. Today there are only some1300 pairs. Outside East Europe they are found in the former USSR, Iran, Turkey, Mongolia and China.

Dalmatian Pelicans are easily disturbed. Some of the reed beds where they nest are harvested by local people. Fishermen also shoot pelicans because they think they take too many fish.

LOGGERHEAD TURTLE
Caretta caretta

◀ Most species of marine turtle are at risk for a variety of reasons. Some people like to eat turtle meat, their shells can be made into ornaments, and the beaches where they lay their eggs are being taken over by tourism.

This is a particular problem in Greece, where the female Loggerhead Turtle attempts to lay her eggs on beaches that were once deserted. Although the Greek government has various laws to protect the turtles, the development goes on.

▲ OLM
Proteus anguinus

This type of salamander lives in underground lakes and streams in the mountains of Europe. It is found from the Alps in south Austria, through northern Italy to the western mountain ranges of Yugoslavia into Dalmatia.

The Olm is currently threatened by pollution, which gets into its underground streams. It is also collected for the specialist pet trade.

▲ *Tourism is a growing threat to Greek wildlife.*

DENMARK

BALTIC
SEA

10°

20°

30°

UKRAINE

Gdańsk

Szczecin

Oder

Vistula

Poznań

POLAND

Warsaw

Łódź

Wrocław

GERMANY

OBE
MOUNTAINS

50°

Prague

CZECH
REPUBLIC

Kraków

Ostrava

CARPATHIAN

MOUNTAINS

50°

Brno

TATRA
MOUNTAINS

SLOVAKIA

Košice

MOLDOVA

Bratislava

AUSTRIA

Miskolc

Danube

Budapest

Debrecen

HUNGARY

Cluj

ROMANIA

SLOVENIA

Lake
Balaton

Hungarian Plain

Mureș

Mt Moldoveanul
(8,348ft/2,548 m)

Brașov

Ljubljana

Zagreb

Pécs

Szeged

Arad

TRANSYLVANIAN ALPS

Ploiești

Rijeka

CROATIA

Drava

Timișoara

Bucharest

Constanța

Sava

BOSNIA

Belgrade

BLACK
SEA

ADRIATIC
SEA

DINARIC

HERZEGOVINA

Sarajevo

SERBIA

Danube

BULGARIA

Varna

ITALY

Split

ALPS

BALKAN

MOUNTAINS

Burgas

Dubrovnik

MONTENEGRO

Sofia

Stara Zagora

10°

Skopje

Plovdiv

Tirana

MACEDONIA

ALBANIA

Vlorë

Korçë

Mt. Olympus
(9,570 ft/2,918 m)

Thessaloniki

AEGEAN
SEA

Lesbos

TURKEY

40°

Corfu

PINDUS MOUNTAINS

GREECE

Chios

40°

Ionian Islands

Patrai

Corinth

Athens

N

W   E

S

Peloponnese

Rhodes

MEDITERRANEAN SEA

Crete

30°

0   500 km

cm 1 2 3 4 5 6 7 8 9 10

inches   1   2   3   4

0   500 miles

The major habitat in this part of the world is desert. Every country in northern Africa has areas of desert, and in some cases these areas are growing. This puts great pressure on animals as they compete with people for scarce natural resources. Tropical forests are also found in North Africa, but they are rapidly being destroyed by local people.

 Few animals can survive in harsh desert conditions.

▼ PYGMY HIPPOPOTAMUS
Choeropsis liberiensis

These shy animals live in the forests and swamps of Liberia, Ivory Coast, Sierra Leone and Guinea. They look like the young of the much bigger, more common, hippopotamus.

Both kinds have to keep their skin moist.

The larger species spends most of the day in rivers or lakes, coming out at night to feed, but since the Pygmy Hippopotamus lives in damp forests, it does not have to spend so much time in the water, although it still likes to wallow in mud.

They feed on roots, plants and fruits, but this food is becoming more and more scarce as the forests are cut down.

◄ ADDAX
Addax nasomaculatus

Once quite widespread over North Africa, there are now only about 5000 of these antelope, in the deserts of south Algeria, west Sudan, Mauritania, Mali, Niger and Chad.

Addax are adapted for desert life. They can travel long distances to find food, and they do not have to drink much water. But they face a number of threats. They are hunted for sport, just because people want their striking horns for trophies; they have to compete with goats for the vegetation they eat; and disturbance from people is forcing them further into the desert where there is little food.

In some countries, the Addax has special protection and is being bred in captivity.

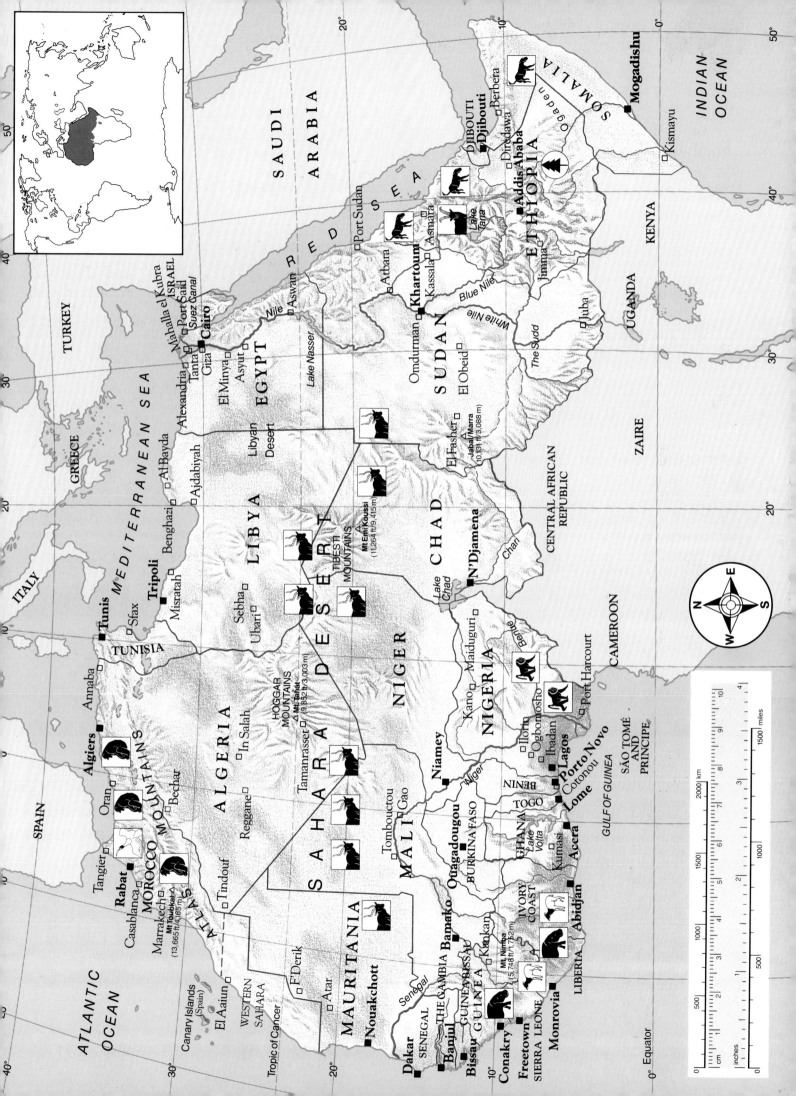

▲ HERMIT IBIS
Geronticus eremita

At one time, this species of ibis could be found living in the mountains of Europe. Today it is only just managing to survive in a handful of small colonies in Morocco, where there are fewer than 400 birds.

Most species of ibis live in areas of wetland, but the Hermit Ibis prefers dry habitats, where it feeds on insects and lizards. The birds nest together on steep rock faces and fly south for the winter.

There was a colony in Turkey but it was gradually surrounded by houses and no birds now remain in the wild there. Captive breeding is probably their only hope.

▲ *War threatens the habitat of the Wild Ass.*

▼ JENTINK'S DUIKER
Cephalophus jentinki

This species of antelope is found only in the lowland forests of Sierra Leone, Liberia and south-west Ivory Coast.

The short front legs, longer back legs, and arched bodies of the duikers make it easy for them to move through thick vegetation, and they get their name from the Afrikaans word meaning diver, as they will dive into the undergrowth to hide.

The rarest of all the duikers, it is threatened by the loss of its forest habitat and by hunting for its skin and meat. A 1979 survey showed that a third of all the game skins in Liberia were Jentink's Duiker skins.

▶ BARBARY MACAQUE
Macaca sylvanus

Also known as the Barbary Ape, this is the only monkey in Africa found north of the Sahara. It was once far more common, but is now found only in a few places in Morocco and Algeria. There is also a semi-captive population that has been introduced to Gibraltar, on the southern tip of Spain.

The gradual destruction of the macaque's natural habitat, over thousands of years, means that it is now under threat. Its habitat started to disappear in the time of the Roman Empire, when the forests in North Africa began to be cut down for timber and fuel.

As more and more land was taken over for farming, the macaques moved to mountainous areas. The forests here are difficult for people to reach, so the macaques were left more or less in peace, but now even these trees are being cut down. Macaques are also being killed because they are thought to be pests that eat the farmers' crops. They are not on

the endangered list yet, but they may be soon if these threats to their existence continue.

DRILL
Mandrillus leucophaeus

Drills are found in the tropical forests of Nigeria, Cameroon and the island of Baccy. The Drill is related to the mandrill, but does not have the well-known, brightly coloured face of the adult male. The two species do not live together as they are separated by the Sanaga river in Cameroon.

Little is known about the way they live in the wild, but Drills are mainly ground dwellers, like the baboons to which they are also related. They live in groups of up to 20 animals and feed on the fruit, leaves and termites of the forest. Because the forest is being cut down, they are losing their habitat, a common problem throughout North Africa.

▼ WALIA IBEX
Capra walie

A member of the goat family, this ibex is perfectly adapted for clambering around the rocky slopes and high cliffs of the Simien Mountains in Ethiopia, now their only habitat.

There are only about 150 left. Hunting used to be the main threat to the Walia Ibex, but the area where it lives is now a national park, patrolled by armed guards.

▲ AFRICAN WILD ASS
Equus africanus

This is the wild ancestor of the donkey. It used to be very common and was found over much of northern Africa. Now it is far less widespread, and is only found in southern Sudan, near the Red Sea coast, in Somalia and also in Ethiopia, where the largest population still survives. By the most recent estimates there are about 3000.

The Wild Ass used to be hunted and captured for collectors who wanted live animals, and local people have always hunted it for food, because it is thought to cure a kind of liver disease called hepatitis. Also, there have been many wars in the area they live in and asses have been killed for food by the soldiers.

The Wild Ass lives in very dry, barren places that are becoming more like a desert all the time. It has to travel far in search of water and this water is often used by herds of domestic animals and their owners, who scare the ass away. The domestic animals also eat the same food as the wild ass, and when the vegetation is in short supply, little is left over for them. The future of this animal does not look good.

Of all the habitats in southern Africa, from baking deserts to steamy swampland, the most famous are the wide, grassy plains called the savannah. Antelopes and zebras graze there in millions, hunted by lions, wild dogs, leopards and cheetahs, but even in such large numbers, the animals are at risk from poachers and farmers.

▲ *African Elephants are brutally killed for their tusks.*

▼ AYE-AYE
Daubentonia madagascariensis

One of the most endangered lemurs, Aye-ayes are hunted because people think they are unlucky, and only a few remain in Madagascar's disappearing rainforest. Since 1990 they have been protected as part of the World Wide Fund for Nature conservation programme on the island.

▲ AFRICAN ELEPHANT
Loxodonta africana

The largest living land animal is under attack from poachers who hunt and kill it just to take its tusks. The tusks, which are in fact enormous front teeth, are made of ivory, and this is often carved to make valuable ornaments and jewellery. In recent years, many countries have agreed to ban imports of ivory, to try and stop elephants being killed. But even in specially protected areas, such as national parks, elephants are still hunted by poachers.

Like all very large animals, elephants take a long time to produce their young. A female cannot breed until she is 14 years old and the pregnancy lasts for two years. Because of this, they cannot breed quickly enough to replace all the elephants that are being killed.

▼ BROWN HYENA
Hyaena brunnae

This is a scavenger from the drier parts of southern Africa. Although hyenas can hunt in packs for their own food, the Brown Hyena prefers to let other animals do the killing, then eat the leftovers.

Although they are still widespread in Namibia and Botswana, they have become rare elsewhere in southern Africa. They have to compete for food with the larger Spotted Hyena, and they are hunted by people because they think they kill their farm animals.

10°   0°

CHAD

Lake Chad

SUDAN

NIGERIA

ETHIOPIA

SOMALIA

ADAMAOUA MOUNTAINS

Mount Cameroon
3,353ft/4,070m

CAMEROON
Douala
Yaounde

Malabo

**CENTRAL AFRICAN
REPUBLIC**

Bangui

Uele

**EQUATORIAL
GUINEA**

Libreville

GABON

Zaire

Kisangani
Boyoma Falls

Kampala

UGANDA

Kisumu

KENYA

*Lake
Turkana*

Mount
Kenya
(17,058ft/5,200m)

Equator

Nairobi

Mombasa

SÃO TOMÉ
AND
PRINCIPE

GULF OF
GUINEA

CONGO

Congo

ZAIRE

Bukavu

RWANDA
Kigali
Bujumbura
BURUNDI

*Lake
Tanganyika*

TANZANIA

Dodoma

Dar es Salaam

**INDIAN
OCEAN**

Zanzibar

Brazzaville

Pointe Noire
CABINDA
(Angola)
Matadi

Kinshasa

Kananga

Mouji-Mayi

Kwango

Kasai

Lualaba

RIFT VALLEY

Aldabra

Luanda

ANGOLA

Likasi
Lubumbashi

*Lake
Bangweula*

*Lake
Malawi*

Ruvuma

Moroni
COMOROS

Antseranana

ATLANTIC
OCEAN

Lobito

Huambo

Kitwe

ZAMBIA

MALAWI
Lilongwe

Moçambique

Lusaka

Zambezi

Cubango

*Victoria
Falls*

Harare

ZIMBABWE

Mutare

Beira

Toamasina

Antananarivo

MADAGASCAR

Okavango
Swamp

NAMIBIA

Francistown

BOTSWANA

Limpopo

MOZAMBIQUE CHANNEL

Windhoek

KALAHARI

DESERT

Namib Desert

WALVIS BAY
(South Africa)

Gaborone

Johannesburg

Pretoria

Maputo
Mbabane
SWAZILAND

REPUBLIC **OF**

Vaal

Welkom

Kimberley
Bloemfontein

Maseru
LESOTHO

Pietermaritzburg
Durban

Orange

Great Karoo

SOUTH AFRICA

Cape Town
Cape of
Good Hope

East London

Port Elizabeth

DRAKENSBERG MOUNTAINS

Tropic of Capricorn

Key to National Parks/Game Reserves
1 Masai Mara National Park
2 Serengeti National Park
3 Amboseli Reserve
4 Kafue National Park
5 Kruger National Park

▼ BLACK RHINOCEROS
Diceros bicornis

Of the two types of African rhinoceros, Black and White, the Black is the most endangered and is protected in many countries, but poachers still hunt it for its horn. Some people think, wrongly, that the horn is a powerful medicine. It is also used to make dagger handles for tribes in the Yemen.

From 1969 to 1977, about 8000 rhinoceroses were killed to make dagger handles, and now only 15,000 Black Rhinoceroses remain.

▲ NILE CROCODILE
Crocodylus niloticus

The Nile Crocodile is found near rivers, lakes and swamps throughout all of Africa.

Crocodiles usually spend the night in the water, where they hunt for fish. Sometimes they join forces to kill large animals such as the hippopotamus. They have been known to attack humans. They are also scavengers, and may eat dead animals.

Crocodiles have lived on the Earth since the time of the dinosaurs, but now their numbers are declining. Nile Crocodiles are hunted by various animals: lions, elephants, leopards and hippopotamuses can kill even quite large crocodiles. But humans are their worst enemy and they have long been hunted for their skin, which is made into shoes, belts and bags.

▼ AFRICAN WILD DOG
Lycaon pictus

The African Wild Dog is an endangered species, even though it can be found over a large part of Africa. Wild dogs live in groups called packs that are very widely spread out. Sometimes there are so few packs that there may be just one for every 2000 sq km. The total world population is probably only about 10,000.

Packs of African Wild Dogs will travel long distances in search of their food. They hunt as a team, and can catch and kill zebras and other animals that are much larger than themselves.

Wild dogs are often destroyed by people, and they also seem to be unhealthy, often suffering from diseases such as distemper. Their main hope for survival is if they can live where people cannot disturb them, such as semi-desert areas or swamps.

▶ OKAPI
Okapia johnstoni

This member of the giraffe family first became known to scientists in 1901. It lives in the rainforests of northern Zaire and is the only forest-living giraffe. It is found only in certain areas, but in those places it is quite common. The Okapi has been protected in Zaire since 1933, but it is still hunted by local people.

The Okapi has a long tongue that helps it to pull the leaves it feeds on off the forest trees. The stripes on its legs are important as camouflage, but they also help the young Okapis to recognise their parents as they follow them through the forest.

▼ COELACANTH
Latimeria chalumnae

Until 1938, the Coelacanth was known only as a fossil. Its remains had been found in rocks that were 70 million years old, and people thought that it had become extinct.

Then one of these strange, heavily-built fish was caught in a fisherman's net off the coast of South Africa. This caused great excitement: the Coelacanth had been living for millions of years around the Comoros Islands. No one knows how many remain, but they are still being caught by fishermen and there may be very few left.

▲ MOUNTAIN GORILLA
Gorilla gorilla beringei

The Mountain Gorilla lives in the mountain rainforest of Zaire, Rwanda and Uganda. It is a rare sub-species of the gorilla. This sub-species probably began its history when, at some point, a group of lowland gorillas went to live in the mountains. Gradually, over many generations, their offspring changed to suit the different conditions.

The Mountain Gorilla's habitat is being taken over for farming and it is killed because it damages crops. Poachers also hunt them because they can sell the animals' heads, hands and feet as souvenirs. The gorillas are now protected at the Virunga Volcano National Park, in Rwanda. They are a great tourist attraction and are therefore more valuable alive than dead.

Three continents meet here: Africa, Asia and Europe. Animals in this region vary greatly because of this, but as much of the land is desert, many of them have to cope with extremely dry conditions.

▼ARABIAN ORYX
Oryx leucoryx

This small, desert-living antelope was hunted to extinction in the wild in the 1960s. The hunters used cars to chase the animals and run them down, so that they could easily be shot and killed.

Fortunately, there were still some animals living in zoos around the world, so a captive breeding programme was started. All the animals were gathered together in one place. The zoo chosen – in Phoenix, Arizona – was selected because the climate there was similar to that of the animals' natural habitat.

The Arabian Oryxes bred and the herd gradually became larger. By the mid-1980s there were enough for some to be returned to the wild. Now, for the first time since they were made extinct in the wild, there are some reintroduced Arabian Oryxes living in various parts of Oman.

▲ CHEETAH
Acinonyx jubatus

This is the fastest animal on four legs – it can run short sprints at speeds of up to 96km/hour (60 mph). This ability is vital to the Cheetah because, unlike the other members of the cat family, it catches its food by outrunning its prey.

Because of their speed, Cheetahs were used by people in Asia as hunting animals, for chasing after prey. Despite this use, the Asian Cheetahs are at even greater risk than those in Africa.

This beautiful animal is endangered because it has been hunted for so many years for its fur coat. It is also threatened by the steady destruction of its natural habitat.

▼MEDITERRANEAN MONK SEAL
Monachus monachus

This seal is under great threat, and there are only 500-700 left. They live mostly in the Aegean and eastern Mediterranean but are also found in the south-west Black Sea, and farther west in the Mediterranean, Adriatic and even the Atlantic.

They are easily disturbed by people, and only breed on beaches hidden inside caves. As the Mediterranean is developed for tourism, there are fewer suitable beaches left for them.

▲ *Open land is giving way to vast oil refineries.*

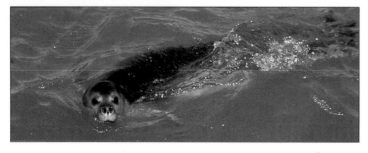

RUSSIA (and its neighbours)

Russia is the largest country in the world. It is the dominant country in the Commonwealth of Independent States (CIS), the new name for the former USSR. Much of the land there is used for growing food. There is also heavy industry, which can create problems for the environment. Large areas are almost unpopulated due to the inhospitable conditions. Much of Siberia, for example, remains unchanged, but in other parts of the CIS animals have suffered at the hands of humans.

EUROPEAN BISON ▶
Bison bonasus

Unlike its relative from North America, this bison lives in forests and not out on the open plains. It is also larger, taller and has longer legs. It eats grasses, ferns, acorns and tree bark.

At the beginning of the twentieth century, there were two protected herds in Russia, but by the 1920s even these had gone. Fortunately, there were six in captivity, and these were brought together and bred. Now there are 2000, and they have been reintroduced to the Bialowieza Forest in Poland and Belorussia.

STELLER'S SEA COW ▶
Hydrodamalis gigas

These huge sea mammals measured 6-9m (20-30ft) in length and weighed up to 6400 kg (14,000lb). They belonged to a group of mammals that includes the manatees and

dugongs, and have the same ancestors as the elephants.

Steller's Sea Cow lived in the Bering Sea and was first discovered in 1741. From then it took just 27 years for this gentle seaweed-eating animal to be hunted to extinction, mainly by sailors, who killed the Sea Cows for food.

▲ *Lake Baikal, in Siberia. Its wildlife is in danger of being poisoned by pollution because of industrial development.*

▲ SIBERIAN WHITE CRANE
Grus leucogeranus

These great cranes arrive in Siberia in May, when they return to their old nest sites and rear just one chick, although they lay two eggs. Most birds nest between the Yana and Kolyma rivers in north-eastern Siberia. They prefer to nest out of sight of each other, and are easily disturbed.

Once breeding is over, they migrate to wetland areas. These cranes may be on the increase. In 1981, 400 birds were found wintering at Lake Poyang in China. By 1987, the number had increased to 1784. Captive breeding, including a joint project between the USA and Russia, is helping to increase their numbers.

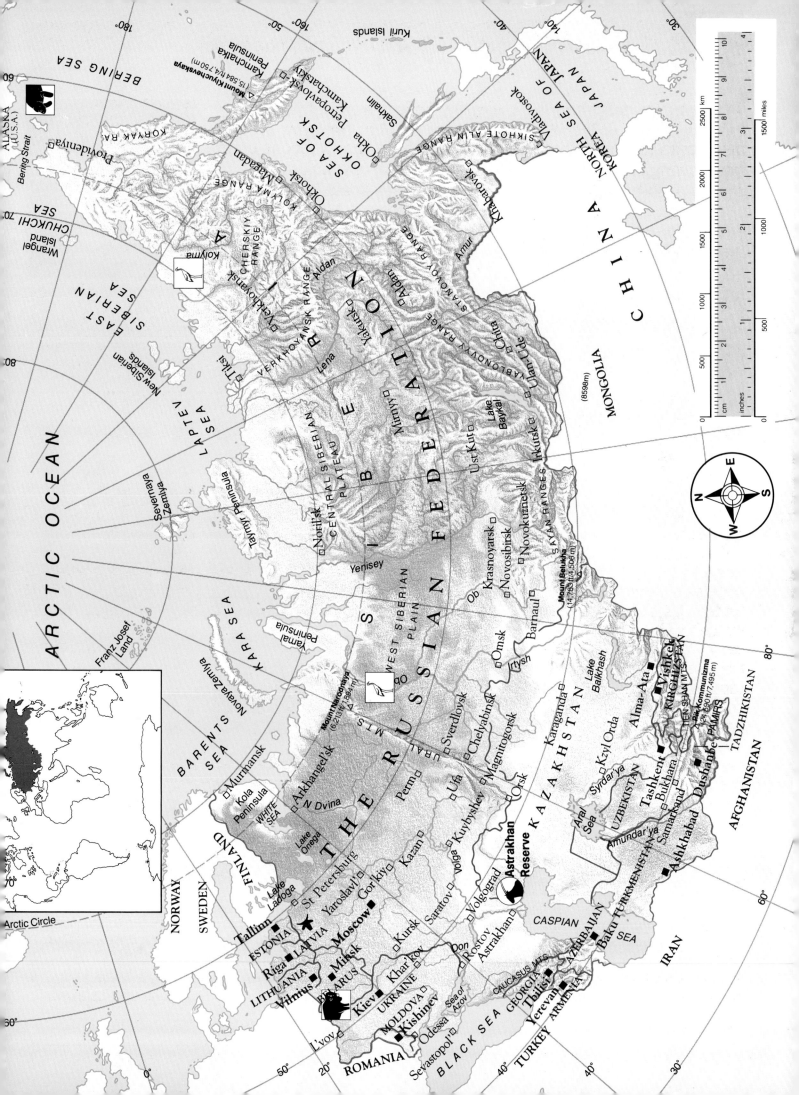

India and its neighbouring countries have a wealth of wildlife, but much of it is in danger. There is a conflict between the needs of the millions of people living here and the needs of wildlife. The range of habitats is very varied, from low-lying swamps and deserts to the world's highest mountains.

► WESTERN TRAGOPAN
Tragopan melanocephalus

This member of the pheasant family lives in forest on the Himalayan mountain sides. The forest here has been cut back by local people and grazed by their animals, and the soil has eroded. There are about 5000 birds left at present.

▲ SNOW LEOPARD
Panthera uncia

This small, light-coloured leopard lives high in the mountains of the Hindu Kush in Afghanistan, and is also found in Tibet and in Siberia.

In summer it has a light, fine coat but in winter it grows a thicker one. It is this fur coat which has been the Snow Leopard's downfall. It is still shot for its fur, although hunting is illegal in some of the countries where it lives.

▲ASIATIC LION
Panthera leo persica

Today, the once-widespread Asiatic Lion has almost died out, and is found only in the Gir Forest National Park. Even now that they are on a reserve, the killing of these lions continues. This is because they eat livestock – and sometimes, people.

▲ TIGER
Panthera tigris

At the beginning of the twentieth century there were 40,000 tigers in India, but by the early 1970s there were less than 1800. Ruthless hunting had reduced their numbers dangerously.

In 1972, 'Operation Tiger' was launched to try and save the tigers of South-East Asia. There are now 17 tiger reserves in India. Although they only protect about a quarter of India's tigers, the reserves have been very successful. In 1984 it was estimated that 4000 tigers were living in India.

CHINA AND JAPAN (and their neighbours)

China is the third largest country in the world, and has the largest population. With so many people to feed, much of the land has been taken over to produce food. This puts a lot of pressure on the wildlife, but the Chinese are very proud of their animals and have reserves and special laws to protect many of their endangered species. However, in such a large country, it is sometimes difficult to make sure that nobody breaks these laws. Japan is a small country made up of four main islands. Because it is so densely populated, and has very intensive industry, wildlife suffers from a lack of space and from pollution.

▲ GIANT PANDA
Ailuropoda melanoleuca

    E

The Giant Panda's ancestors were all meat eaters, but over millions of years it has changed its diet to bamboo shoots, and now eats little else. This meant that when the bamboo died out in the 1980s (because people were felling bamboo forests to grow crops), at least 150 pandas starved to death. Captive breeding has been difficult, but it may be their only real chance for survival.

▶ BIET'S SNUB-NOSED MONKEY
Pygathrix (Rhinopithecus) bieti

   E

This is the least well known of the four species of snub-nosed monkeys. All except the Golden Snub-nosed Monkey are endangered.

Biet's Snub-nosed Monkey lives in the mountains of Yunnan Province. In the 1960s there were about 800 living there, but no one knows current numbers.

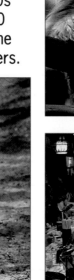

▲ PRZEWALSKI'S HORSE
Equus przewalskii

  Ex

This horse was first discovered by a Western naturalist in 1878, but about 80 years later it was extinct in the wild. As people moved into its habitat, they brought their own horses. The Przewalski stallions may have bred with some of the domestic mares, until their own special characteristics were lost. Settlers may also have killed the stallions when trying to take the mares away to breed with their own horses.

▲ *The Japanese take a lot of their food from the sea*

Fortunately, some Przewalski's Horses had been bred in captivity and today there are about 800. In the 1980s, a breeding programme was set up in China so the horses could be reintroduced into the wild.

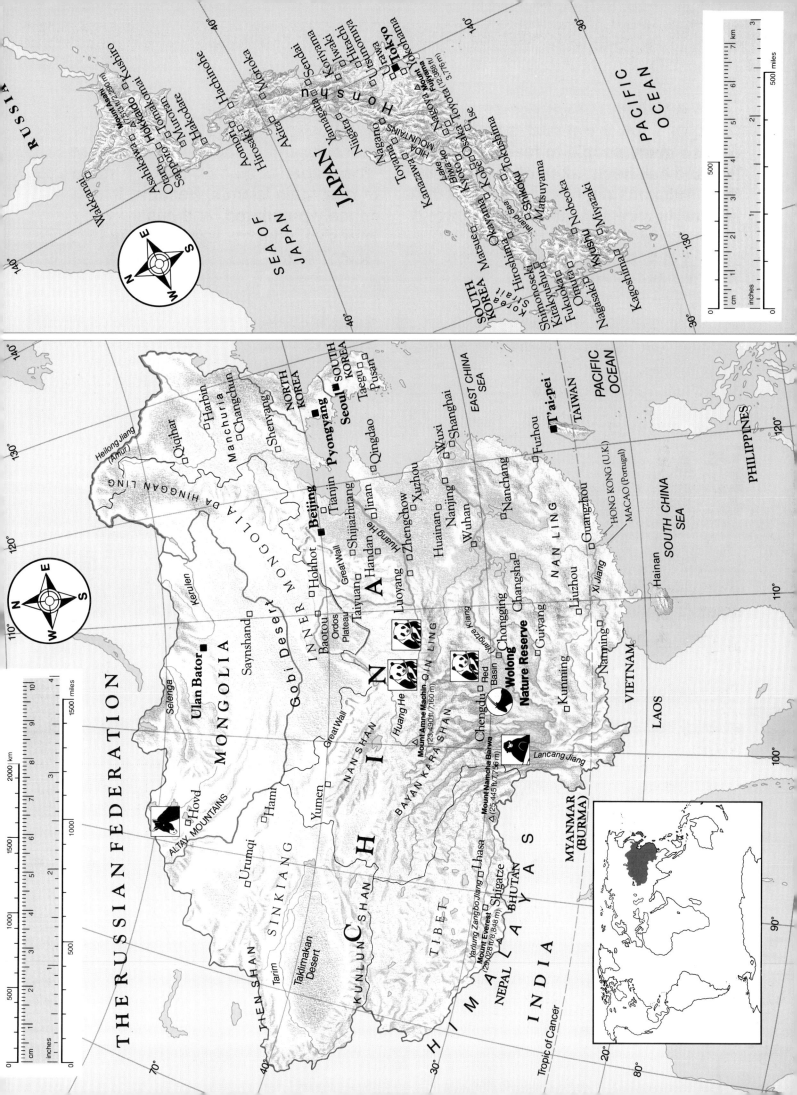

There are thousands of islands of different sizes in this part of the world, and a huge variety of wildlife. Much of the region used to be covered in tropical rainforest, but in recent times a lot of it has been cut down. On the mainland there has been war and strife for the people of Vietnam and Kampuchea, and wildlife has suffered too.

▲ War in Vietnam has devastated the environment.

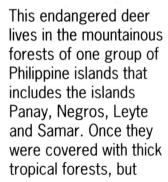

◀ ORANG-UTAN

Pongo pygmaeus

This ape is under pressure everywhere it lives. During the 1960s, their numbers were very badly affected because they were being caught in the wild for the pet trade and zoos. Only the young were ever taken, which meant shooting the mother out of the trees and trying to catch the young ape as it fell. This horrible practice must have resulted in many young animals dying too, but no one can even guess how many.

Although most zoos breed their own Orang-utans now, there is still a trade in live animals caught in the wild. In Sabah, they are hunted for food and sport. It is difficult to work out how many survive. There are 180,000 living in Sumatra and Kalimantan. Perhaps only 20,000 live in protected reserves. The main danger is from logging and tree-felling in the forests where Orang-utans live.

▶ PHILIPPINE SPOTTED DEER

Cervus alfredi

This endangered deer lives in the mountainous forests of one group of Philippine islands that includes the islands Panay, Negros, Leyte and Samar. Once they were covered with thick tropical forests, but people have cleared over half of the forest for timber or farming.

The biggest population of this deer lives on Panay. A project to breed them in captivity there was going well until terrorists raided the area and the five deer were all killed. The deer is already extinct on two of the islands. Its chances are poor unless it is taken into captivity to be bred.

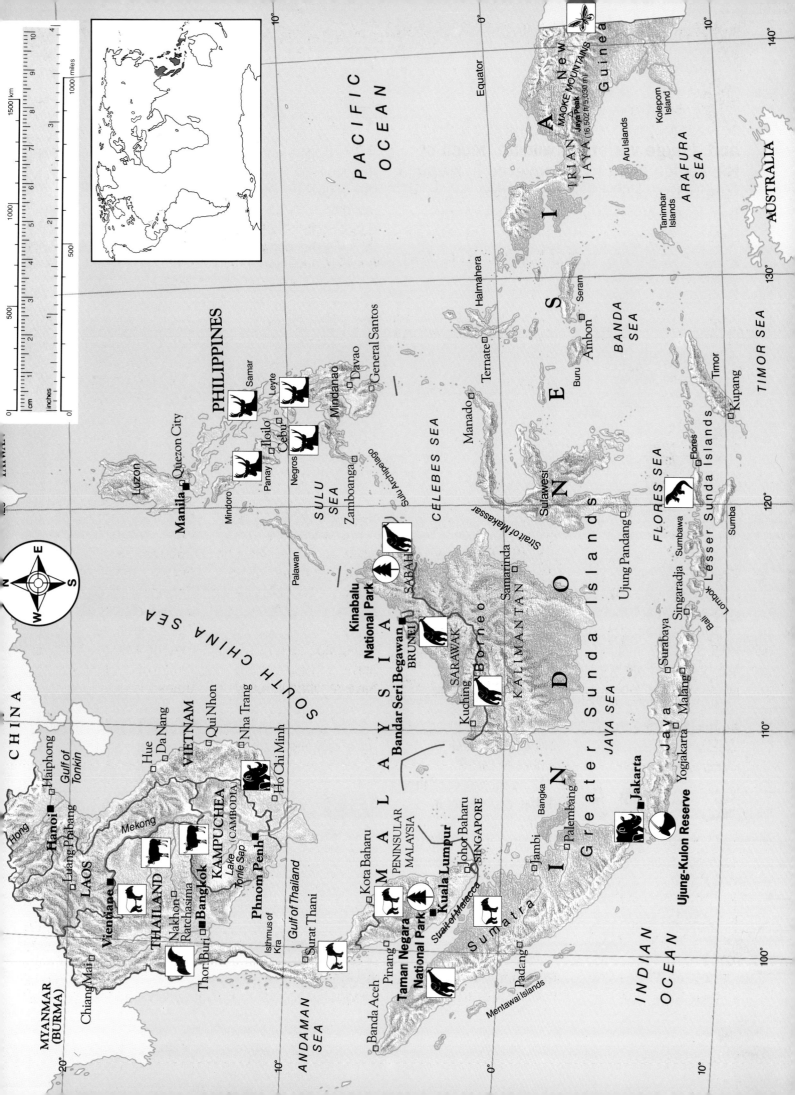

◄ KITTI'S HOG-NOSED BAT
Craseonycteris thonglongyai

Kitti's Hog-nosed Bat is the smallest mammal in the world. This tiny bat weighs from 1.5–3g (about one fifteenth of an ounce), the size of a large bumblebee. This is why it is also called a Bumblebee Bat. They were first discovered in 1974, living in limestone caves in Thailand, and roosting high up on the caves' roofs.

The area where they live has been cleared for agriculture and only about 200 bats are left living in a few caves in one area of Thailand. The greatest danger is from collectors interested in obtaining specimens, dead or alive.

▼ QUEEN ALEXANDRA'S BIRDWING BUTTERFLY
Ornithoptera alexandrae

The world's largest butterfly is also the most threatened. It lives in about 1000 sq km (386 sq miles) of forest in northern Papua New Guinea. The male's 25-cm (10-in) wing span and glowing colours make it a popular decoration. Its forest habitat is also being taken over by oil palm growers. There are plans to ranch the butterfly, so it can be sold without harming the natural population.

▲ KOMODO DRAGON
Varanus komodoensis

This is the largest lizard in the world, and it commonly grows to a length of 3m (10ft), while the biggest on record was 3.2m (10.5ft). The Komodo Dragon lives only on a few Indonesian islands.

Because the dragons often try to eat villagers' livestock, and have eaten people, local people try to kill them. However, the Indonesian government have made it illegal to kill the dragons, and now tourists come to see them, which brings money to the islands. There are about 5000 dragons alive today.

▲ *Palau Langkawi island, off western Malaysia.*

◀ JAVAN RHINOCEROS
Rhinoceros sondaicus

This is one of the most endangered species of rhinoceros in the world. There are only about 60 left. Fifty of them live in the Ujong Kulon reserve in western Java. The others live in a reserve in Vietnam, 130km (80 miles) north-east of Ho Chi Minh City. They were discovered there in 1989 after a hunter shot one and was later arrested.

At one time, this rhinoceros was found from Bangladesh, through Burma, Thailand and throughout Indonesia, but like the other two Asian rhinoceroses, it has been hunted for its horns. The people of the region think the horn is a powerful medicine, but there is no evidence that it is.

▼ KOUPREY
Bos sauveli

The Kouprey is a member of the cattle tribe. It was discovered by scientists in 1937, when there were thought to be no more than 1000. Since then conditions in Kampuchea, where it is mostly found, have got worse. After years of war in the area, people had given up hope of finding any alive. But in July 1982, a small herd was seen in eastern Thailand, and a captive breeding programme has now been proposed.

▼ MALAYAN TAPIR
Tapirus indicus

Tapirs are an ancient group of animals, related both to horses and rhinoceroses. All the other species of tapir are found in South America.

They have a long snout which they use to feed from different plants in the forest or near rivers. Although it is found over a large area, in Burma, Thailand, Malaya and Sumatra, it is in danger. It is hunted for sport, for food and for its skin. Its habitat is also being destroyed by growing development.

The Australian continent is home to some of the world's strangest mammals – marsupials. They are born in a fairly undeveloped state, and then develop in their mother's pouch. Marsupials lived undisturbed for many years, but since the first settlers arrived about 200 years ago they have been in danger.

Before settlers arrived in New Zealand, the native animals were well adapted to their environment. But once new animals were introduced, the balance of nature was threatened.

▲ The distinctive red desert of Western Australia.

▲ LEADBEATER'S POSSUM
Gymnobelideus leadbeateri

This little tree-living marsupial was first discovered in 1867 in the Bass River Valley, in the State of Victoria. Five were collected over about 30 years, but then nothing more of this animal was seen.

By 1921, its habitat of rainforest and scrub had been almost entirely destroyed by settlers, so it seemed that there was little chance of its survival. It was thought that this possum had become extinct before anyone had found anything out about it.

Then in 1961, it was spotted at a tourist spot only 110km (68 miles) from the city of Melbourne. Surveys showed that it was still living in the mountainous Central Highland Zone, in Victoria. The ash trees growing there were a favourite place for it to shelter. Today it is at risk once again from forest clearance and bad management of its woodland habitat.

▼ SALTWATER CROCODILE
Crocodylus porosus

This species of crocodile can swim in the sea, so it is found all over South-East Asia, as well as on the northern coast of Australia.

It is the largest species of crocodile in the world (and the world's largest living reptile), and it can grow as long as 7m (23ft). It has a reputation for being a man-eater, as it has killed people who got too close to the crocodile-infested creeks and rivers of Australia.

Despite this reputation, it is a protected species. Its numbers were dangerously reduced by hunting in the past. Like all crocodiles, it has been killed for its skin.

◀ TUATARA
Sphenodon punctatus

As New Zealand is so isolated, Tuataras have hardly changed since the time of the dinosaurs. They are found only on small islands off South Island, where they shelter in the nesting burrows of various seabirds. When rats arrived in New Zealand and started eating these birds' young, there were fewer burrows for the Tuatara.

▼ NUMBAT
Myrmecobius fasciatus

▶ KAKAPO
Strigops habroptilus

The Numbat is a small marsupial that eats only termites.

There used to be many Numbats in southern and central Australia, but today they are found only in woodland in the south-west of Western Australia. Most of their habitat has been turned over to farming, and they are preyed on by foxes, cats and dogs introduced from Europe by settlers.

This large, flightless parrot was once common in most of New Zealand, because it had no natural predators.

Disaster struck when settlers came, bringing dogs, rats, cats, stoats and ferrets. By the early 1970s it was thought to be as good as extinct, because only male birds were left. But in 1977, 30 males were found on Stewart Island. In 1981,

a female was found there, and in 1982, two nests. Over the next few years males and females were found and numbers rose to an estimated 200.

▲ Red Deer: one of the introduced species causing problems for New Zealand's original animals.

▶ THYLACINE
Thylacinus cynocephalus

Although this marsupial is thought to be extinct, some scientists hope that it may be rediscovered living in the thick Tasmanian forests.

When, in the 1800s, European settlers came to Tasmania with their sheep, they thought the Thylacines would prey on their flocks – this was probably because it looked like a wolf – and so the persecution of this poor animal began. Between 1888 and 1914, at least 2268

Thylacines were deliberately killed, and in 1910, a disease brought in by the settlers' dogs killed most of the remaining Thylacines. What was likely to have been the last Thylacine was captured in 1933 and died in Hobart Zoo

three years later.

In 1985, someone said they saw a Thylacine in Western Australia, where it is supposed to have been extinct for 1000 years. But, as with a more recent sighting in Tasmania, the evidence is not very convincing.

▼ NORTHERN HAIRY-NOSED WOMBAT
Lasiorhinus krefftii

Wombats are closely related to the Koala. A major difference is that wombats are burrowing animals, not tree-dwellers like Koalas. The common wombat is often considered to be a pest, because when it burrows it sometimes knocks over the fences that are built to keep rabbits out of grazing land.

There are only about 60 Hairy-nosed Wombats left in Australia, in mid-eastern Queensland.

▲ TAKAHE
Notornis mantelli

From 1898 until 1948, this large, flightless bird was thought to be extinct. Fortunately, it was rediscovered living in the mountainous Lake District of South Island.

This area is protected, but Takahes are also

threatened by animals introduced by settlers. Stoats brought in to kill mice eat their eggs and young, while Red Deer compete with them for the same food. Captive breeding has recently proved successful and Takahes have been released into the wild. Numbers have increased from 120 in 1983 to 260 in August 1990.

THE PACIFIC ISLANDS

The Pacific Ocean covers a third of the Earth, and there are thousands of islands there. Animals reached these islands in different ways – some flew, some drifted and some 'sailed' on rafts of vegetation. But when people settled on the islands they sometimes destroyed the special habitats or brought animals of their own that competed with the native wildlife.

▲ Coral island, Polynesia.

► GALAPAGOS GIANT TORTOISE
Geochelone elephantopus

Of the 14 different tortoise sub-species that have lived on the Galapagos Islands, four are extinct and five are very close to extinction.

For hundreds of years, these animals were hunted for food by sailors, and when people settled on the islands, the problems increased. Their livestock, such as goats, eat the same plants as the tortoises, their dogs attack them, and their pigs eat the tortoise's eggs (as do introduced rats).

▼ CRESTED HONEYCREEPER
Palmeria dolei

This is one of many threatened birds that live on the islands of Hawaii. It is found only on the island of Maui, in a narrow strip of wet forest on the Haleakala volcano, where Ohia trees grow.

It has a straight, pointed beak that it uses for eating insects and nectar from Ohia-lehua trees.

◄ PARTULA SNAIL
Partula tohiveana

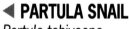

Seven species of this snail lived on Moorea, one of the Society Islands. They are important for scientific research, and are being bred in zoos all over the world – 4000 now

exist in captivity.

They are extinct in the wild due to competition from a carnivorous snail. This carnivorous snail was introduced to eat yet another type of snail, the Giant African Land Snail, that had been introduced earlier, and was eating crops. Unfortunately, the carnivorous snail ate the Partula Snails too.

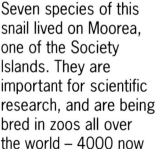

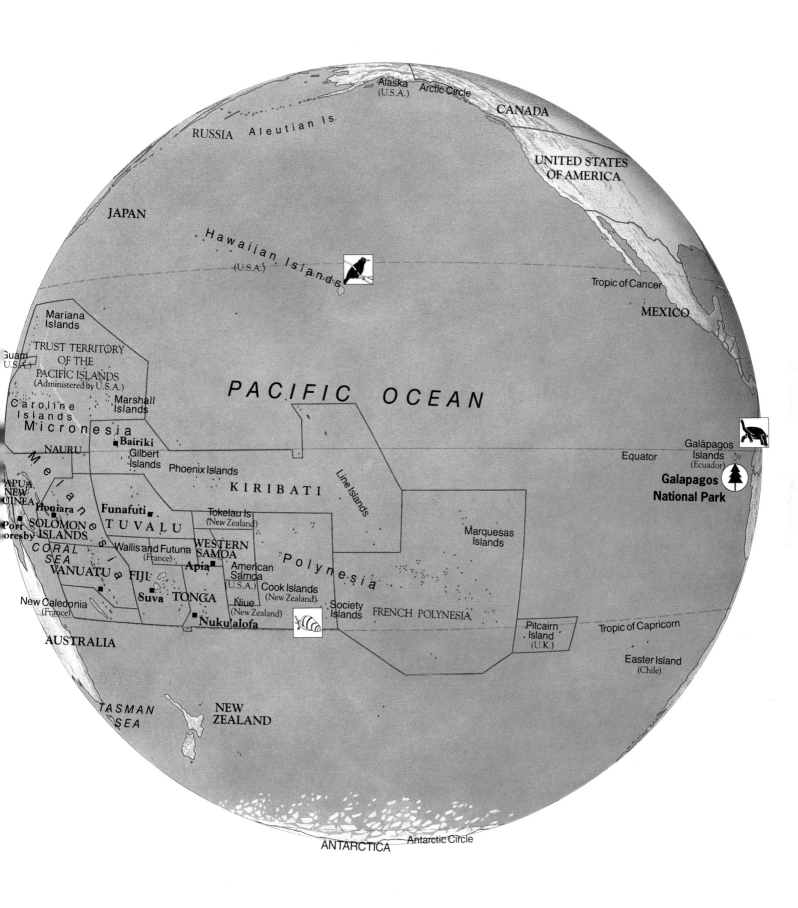

The frozen Arctic is, surprisingly, home to many different animals adapted to the cold environment. Much of the Arctic is frozen, but in the summer plants grow and numerous insects hatch out. The greatest risk to the region is oil pollution, following the recent discovery of oil here.

▲ *Summer in the Arctic.*

▶ LAPTEV WALRUS
Odobenus rosmarus laptevi

The Walrus is found in the Arctic Ocean and in nearby seas. It is one sub-species, known as the Laptev Walrus, that is included in the IUCN listings, and there are thought to be less than 10,000 left.

For over 200 years, Walruses were hunted for their tusks, skin and oil. They nearly became extinct 100 years ago. Today they are only hunted by local people, – as many as 12,000 a year are being taken by Alaskan Inuit for ivory from the tusks. If local hunting continues at this rate, the Walrus will soon be in real danger.

▲ NARWHAL
Monodon monoceros

This member of the whale family is unusual because of its long, single tusk. Only the male Narwhals have this tusk, which is actually a tooth. Narwhals only have two teeth and it is the left one which grows in this way. No one is sure what the tusk is used for, but it is thought that males use it for fighting and to show who is dominant.

Narwhals have always been hunted for their skin, fat and tusks. Today, there are less than 20,000 left and a certain number are allowed to be hunted. For example, 500 Narwhals may be hunted in Canada each year.

▲ *An operation to clear up an oil spill.*

▲ *The male Arctic fox blends in with the snow in his white winter coat; the coat turns grey in summer.*

Antarctica belongs to no one. Nobody lives there permanently and while seals, penguins and seabirds stop off here to breed, no large animals live there. Many countries have research stations in the Antarctic and an international treaty has, so far, prevented it from being exploited.

▲ *Leith Harbour Whaling Station, South Georgia.*

▼ BLUE WHALE
Balaenoptera musculus

The Blue Whale has been hunted for years, first of all in the north Atlantic, then in the Antarctic too.

The most important by-products were the oils from the whales' blubber (fat under the skin) which were used for making foods such as margarine. The Antarctic island of South Georgia became the centre of the whaling industry. In just one season in 1930-31, 29,000 Blue Whales were slaughtered.

By 1965, the number of Blue Whales had dropped to 6000. Today, it is fully protected, but its numbers are rising very slowly. This may be to do with its food supply. Blue Whales eat a small shrimp-like animal called krill. But so do seals and penguins. When the whales were so reduced by hunting, there was more krill for these other creatures to eat, and their numbers rose. Now there may not be enough for the Blue Whale, especially if plans to exploit krill for feeding humans and livestock get underway.

▲ *The members of a New Zealand research station.*

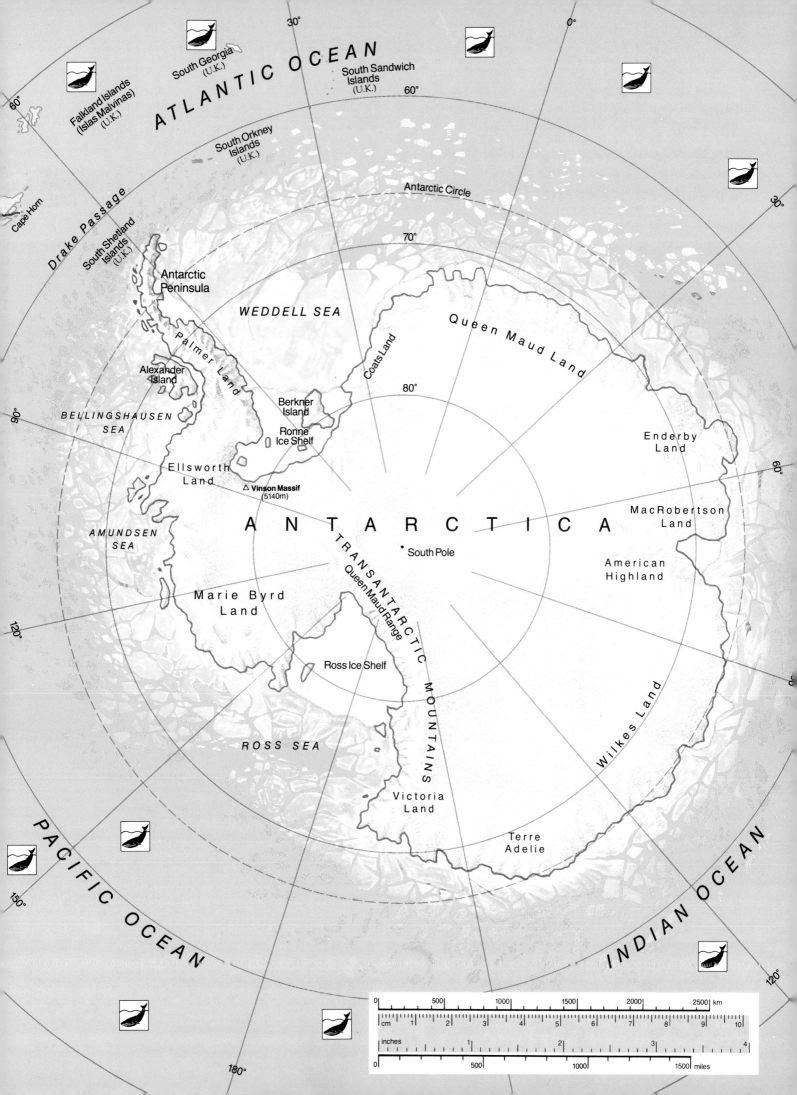

ATLANTIC OCEAN

Falkland Islands
(Islas Malvinas)
(U.K.)

South Georgia
(U.K.)

South Sandwich
Islands
(U.K.)

South Orkney
Islands
(U.K.)

Cape Horn

Drake Passage

South Shetland
Islands
(U.K.)

Antarctic
Peninsula

Antarctic Circle

WEDDELL SEA

Coats Land

Queen Maud Land

Palmer Land

Alexander
Island

Berkner
Island

Ronne
Ice Shelf

Enderby
Land

BELLINGSHAUSEN
SEA

Ellsworth
Land

△ Vinson Massif
(5140m)

MacRobertson
Land

ANTARCTICA

AMUNDSEN
SEA

• South Pole

American
Highland

Marie Byrd
Land

TRANSANTARCTIC

Queen Maud Range

Ross Ice Shelf

MOUNTAINS

Wilkes Land

ROSS SEA

Victoria
Land

PACIFIC OCEAN

Terre
Adelie

INDIAN OCEAN

0		500		1000		1500		2000		2500	km
cm	1	2	3	4	5	6	7	8	9	10	
inches			1		2		3		4		
0		500		1000		1500	miles				

GLOSSARY AND FURTHER INFORMATION

Here are simple explanations of some of the main terms used throughout the book.

Adaptation The process by which living things become suited to their particular environment.

Captivity Animals in captivity are in zoos or other conditions controlled by people. Sometimes they are kept there as part of a captive breeding programme. The aim of this is to breed enough endangered animals so that they can be safely introduced back into the wild.

Competition This happens when one kind of animal wants the same things – such as food – as another animal. In nature there is normally a balance, but when people introduce a new animal to an area, the animals that were there first cannot always compete for resources with the new animal and may become extinct.

Conservation The protection and management of the natural world.

Environment The surroundings and circumstances – type of land, climate, other animals and plants and so on – that an animal or plant lives in.

Evolution The process by which plants and animals change over time to fit in with, and make the most of, their surroundings. Sometimes it takes millions of years. For example, long ago, certain birds landed on the remote islands of New Zealand. Because there were no animals there that attacked these birds, they had no need to fly away from danger and began to stay on the ground. Much later, thousands, or perhaps millions, of years later, the offspring of these first birds could no longer fly.

Extinction The process by which a species of animal or plant dies out altogether. Once this happens, the animal or plant can never be brought back – extinction is forever.

Family A group of similar animals, containing several similar species.

Habitat A specific kind of area where a particular animal or plant naturally lives or grows.

Habitat Destruction The destruction of natural habitats by people. The habitat changes so the animals and plants living there no longer have a natural home.

Hunting When one animal kills another for food. When people hunt animals, it is often not just for food. It can be for the skin of an animal, for sport, a living animal for research, or for the pet trade.

National Park An officially protected place where the environment can be looked after without it being changed or damaged by people. In most national parks, people are welcome, and may actually be a part of the way the park works.

Nature/Game Reserve An area where animals and plants are protected from disturbance by people.

Pollution The process of putting poisonous substances into the environment. For example getting rid of chemicals produced by industry by putting them into rivers.

Ranching Where animals and their young are reared in conditions controlled by people, like farming. Many different kinds of animals have been ranched, for example butterflies, crocodiles and turtles. In many cases ranching stops people taking animals from the wild.

Species A group of animals or plants which can be grouped together because they are very similar and can breed with each other. Several species make up a family.

Sub-species A group of animals or plants within a single species that live in different places or look slightly different from other members of that species.

FURTHER INFORMATION

The following organisations are actively involved in helping to protect animals all over the world. You can write to them for further information.

Young Peoples' Trust for
  the Environment and
  Nature Conservation
95 Woodbridge Road
Guildford
Surrey GU1 4PY

Friends of the Earth
26-28 Underwood Street
London N1 7JQ

Watch Trust for
  Environmental Education
22 The Green
Nettleham
Lincoln LN2 2NR

Fauna & Flora Preservation
  Society (FFPS)
1 Kensington Gore
London SW7 2AR

Young People's Trust for
  Endangered Species
19 Quarry Street
Guildford
Surrey GU1 3EH

Greenpeace
30-31 Islington Green
London N1 8BR

Marine Conservation
  Society
9 Gloucester Road
Ross-on-Wye HR9 5BU

World Wide Fund For
  Nature (WWF)
Panda House
Weyside Park
Catteshall Lane
Godalming
Surrey GU7 1XR

Royal Society for the
  Protection of Birds
The Lodge
Sandy
Bedfordshire
SG19 2DL

MAP INDEX

INDEX OF ANIMALS AND NATIONAL PARKS